MY VICTORY WON

A Meditation on the Hymn, "Be Thou My Vision"

By Todd Stalter (ASCAP)

*M*y Victory Won, by Todd Stalter, explores melodic and metaphorical aspects of the hymn tune "Be Thou My Vision." Taking inspiration from the little-known third verse of the hymn, the bold, percussive introduction soon gives way to a contemplative section featuring unique and interesting timbres and a passage for solo flute. The work ends in a triumphant, unabashed burst of energy and affirmation.

Instrumentation

1 — Conductor Score
5 — 1st Flute
5 — 2nd Flute
2 — Oboe
2 — Bassoon
4 — 1st B♭ Clarinet
4 — 2nd B♭ Clarinet
4 — 3rd B♭ Clarinet
2 — B♭ Bass Clarinet
2 — 1st E♭ Alto Saxophone
2 — 2nd E♭ Alto Saxophone
2 — B♭ Tenor Saxophone
2 — E♭ Baritone Saxophone
3 — 1st B♭ Trumpet
3 — 2nd B♭ Trumpet
3 — 3rd B♭ Trumpet

2 — 1st F Horn
2 — 2nd F Horn
2 — 1st Trombone
2 — 2nd Trombone
2 — 3rd Trombone
2 — Euphonium
2 — Euphonium T.C.
4 — Tuba
Percussion — 7 players:
2 — Mallet Percussion 1
   (Chimes/Bells)
2 — Mallet Percussion 2
   (Vibraphone)
2 — Percussion 1
   (Snare Drum, Bass Drum)
9 — Percussion 2
   (Gong/Mark Tree/Finger
   Cymbals/Tom-Toms [2]/
   Woodblock, Suspended
   Cymbal/Triangle/China
   Cymbal/Cabasa)
2 — Timpani

SUPPLEMENTAL and WORLD PARTS
available for download from www.alfred.com/supplemental

E♭ Alto Clarinet
E♭ Contra Alto Clarinet
B♭ Contra Bass Clarinet
1st E♭ Horn
2nd E♭ Horn
1st Trombone in B♭ T.C.
2nd Trombone in B♭ T.C.
3rd Trombone in B♭ T.C.
1st Trombone in B♭ B.C.
2nd Trombone in B♭ B.C.
3rd Trombone in B♭ B.C.
Euphonium in B♭ B.C.
Tuba in B♭ T.C.
Tuba in B♭ B.C.
Tuba in E♭ T.C.
Tuba in E♭ B.C.
String Bass

Commissioned by the Normal, IL Unit 5 Band Programs and Music Parents,
in honor of Lance Meadows and his career as a Music Educator

My Victory Won

A meditation on the hymn *Be Thou My Vision*

By Todd Stalter (ASCAP)

FULL SCORE
Duration - 3:50

49520S

*Purchase a full-length
performance recording!*
alfred.com/downloads

49520S

13

49520S

18

49520S